TRAUM
TEACHES
Essential
Chords and Progressions for
Acoustic Guitar

Back Cover Photo by Dion Ogust

Audio Editor: Tom Mark

Produced by Artie Traum and Tom Mark
for Homespun Tapes at Make Believe Ballroom, Shokan, NY

ISBN 0-7935-8858-8

HOMESPUN® Tapes

EXCLUSIVELY DISTRIBUTED BY

HAL•LEONARD® CORPORATION
7777 W. BLUEMOUND RD. P.O. BOX 13819 MILWAUKEE, WI 53213

Visit Hal Leonard Online at **www.halleonard.com**

Visit Homespun Tapes on the internet at **http://www.homespuntapes.com**

CD instruction makes it easy! Find the section of the lesson you want with the press of a finger; play that segment over and over until you've mastered it; easily skip over parts you've already mastered—no clumsy rewinding or fast forwarding to find your spot; listen with the best possible audio fidelity; follow along track-by-track with the book.

GUITAR

Artie
TRAUM
TEACHES

Essential
Chords and
Progressions for
Acoustic
Guitar

Table of Contents

1 Introduction

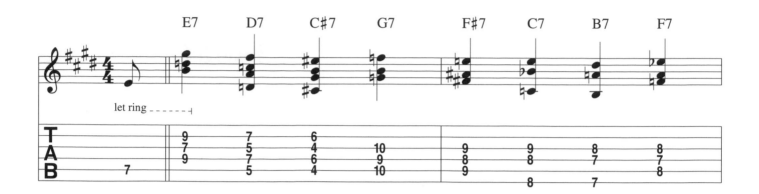

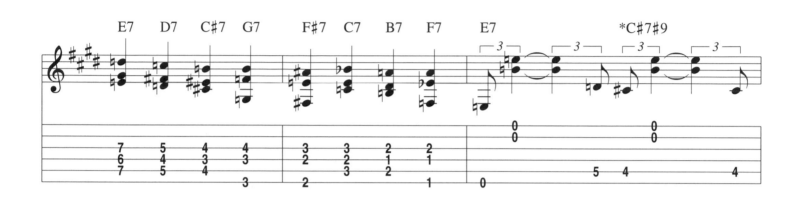

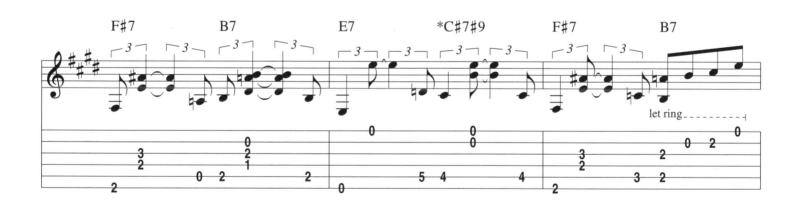

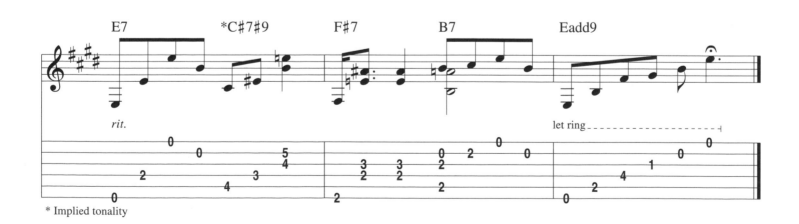

* Implied tonality

Everybody seems to play the basic chords.

The C Chord

The F Chord

The G Chord

The D Chord

One of the things that you can do to these chords is to add 6ths, 9ths, and 7ths so that you can have a full complement of sounds. For example, here's your basic C chord.

If you were to add your pinky to the second string, third fret (the D note), you would have a Cadd9.

The same idea applies to an Am chord.

If you were to remove your second finger from the second fret on the G string, you would get an Am7 chord.

Am7

And by adding your pinky to the third fret on the E string you get an additional Am7 voicing with the seventh in two different places.

Am7

So let's review: Cadd9 and Am7.

Cadd9   Am7

When you play some of these chords, some of the notes won't work very well. For example, in the C chord, the low E won't work.

C/E

So you either have to mute it or play the chord from the fifth string.

As we add notes to chords, bear in mind that we have to be aware of which note we are adding.

So continuing on, we have Cadd9, Am7, Dm, G.

Cadd9   Am7   Dm   G

◆4 Making It Interesting – Cadd9 – Am7 – Dm7 – Gsus

Now to make it a little more interesting, here is your Cadd9, Am7, Dm7, Gsus.

Cadd9   Am7   Dm7   Gsus

◆ 5 ◆ D – D/F# – G – A7 and Right-hand Techniques

Now moving along with this idea, let's jump to D.

In this chord once again, you can't hit the low E string when you strum the chord because it doesn't work.

So you have to start on the D root and then strum the D chord above it.

Now with your D chord in place, reach over with your thumb to the second fret on the sixth string and play the note. Here you get a D/F#.

This is a very important chord and a great passing chord going to G.

A lot of people play the G chord with an open second string.

I really like the G chord with a closed second string.

The V chord of that progression would be an A7.

I prefer doing that as an A7sus4.

A7sus4

And then back to D.

D

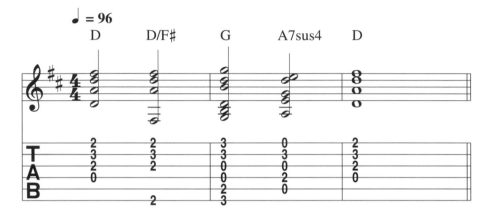

In my right hand I pluck all of the notes.

In the same manner of adding and removing notes, if you take your D chord and remove your third finger from the E string you get a D chord with an open E on top (Dsus2).

Dsus2

Dsus2   D

Then you can add your pinky for a Dsus (Dsus4).

Dsus4

Dsus4   Dsus2   D   Dsus4

Then you can add your fourth finger to the first string on the fifth fret for a D chord with an A on top (DaddA).

DaddA

So you have:

Dsus2   D   Dsus4   DaddA

6 D – Bm7 – Em7 – Asus – Easy Three-note Chords

Now very often a progression will go from D,

D

to Bm which is normally done with a barre.

Bm

Here is another Bm chord (Bm7).

Bm7

But it is played with three notes.

Bm7

So to be very precise, the D chord is like this:

D

The Bm7 sounds like this:

Then you would go to an Em chord. The normal Em chord looks like this:

When you take this form and add your pinky to the second string, third fret (D), you get an Em7 chord.

And then you can end up on the Asus.

Which can take you nicely back to D.

So you have D.

Bm7 as a three-note chord.

A one note change to make Em7.

Completing the cycle with Asus.

Asus

So you can strum it.

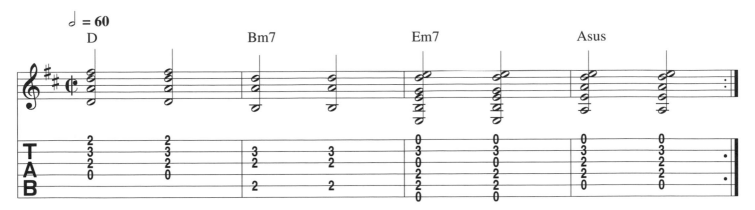

◆7 Arpeggios and Choice of Bass Notes

You can also play these in an arppegiated fashion.

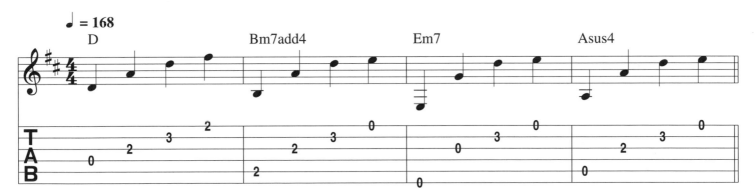

Notice that your choice of bass notes is important.

D in the bass.

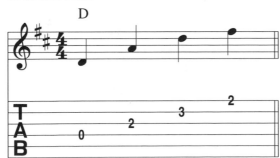

B in the bass

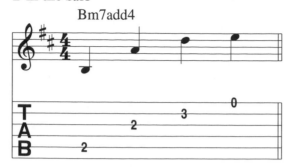

Low E in the bass

And A in the bass

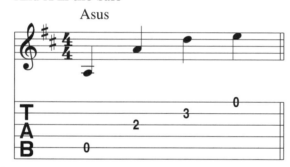

We have all heard this before and it is a beautiful progression.

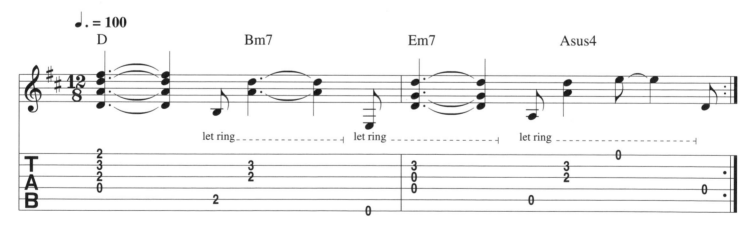

◆ 8 Variation – Em9

Now just to complicate matters a bit more, instead of an Em7,

Em7

you can add your third finger to the second fret of the first string (F♯) and play Em9.

Em9

This chord can be used in both the keys of D Major and E Minor.

So now we have:

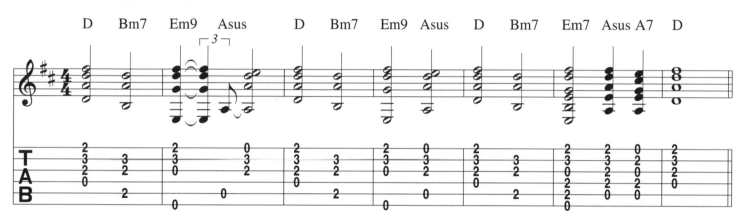

What I did that last time was when I got to the Asus,

Asus

I resolve by just going to an A7,

A7

and then back to D.

D

◆9 D as Drone/Progressions

By using the open D string, you can create an interesting drone effect by playing different chords over the resonating D string drone. For example, from the D chord,

D

you can move to an Em7 chord in 2nd position,

Em/D

and then move that form up two frets,

F♯m/D

and then move it back down two frets.

Em7/D

So it's D, Em/D, F♯m/D, Em/D and then back to D.

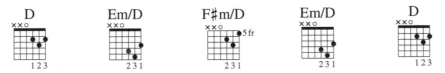

So we have:

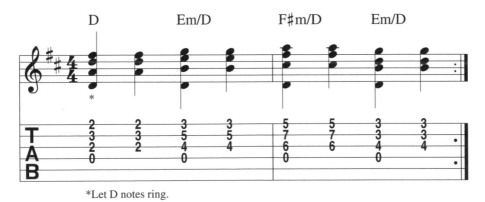

*Let D notes ring.

Now instead of going to the minor chord you can play the minor seventh chord,

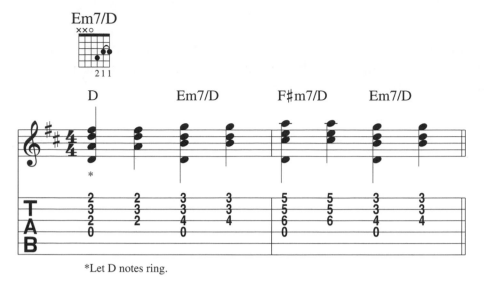

*Let D notes ring.

you can extend it by going upwards,

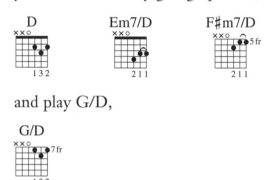

and play G/D,

G/D

and then back down.

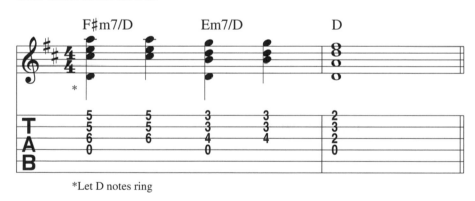

*Let D notes ring

When you start thinking of it rhythmically with some ideas in your right hand you get:

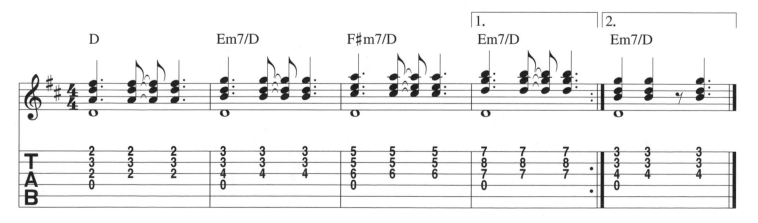

The other nice thing about D is some of the minor chords that come off of it. So as you are working your way up the neck, you can use different bass notes to make this sound a little more interesting. You have your D,

D

going to this new form of an Em7 chord with a B in the bass,

Em7/B

then you can play the same chord with the note A on the G string.

Em11/B

Then you can finish the progression by moving to A7 back to D.

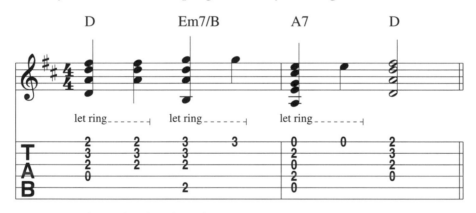

You can take it further by playing a F#m7/C#.

F#m7/C#

So the progression would be as follows:

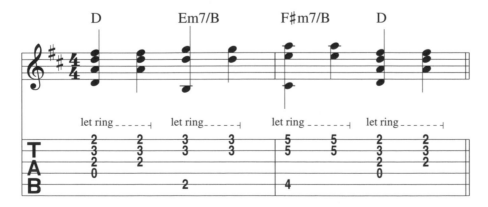

To continue that progression I would go to Bm, Em, Asus, back to D.

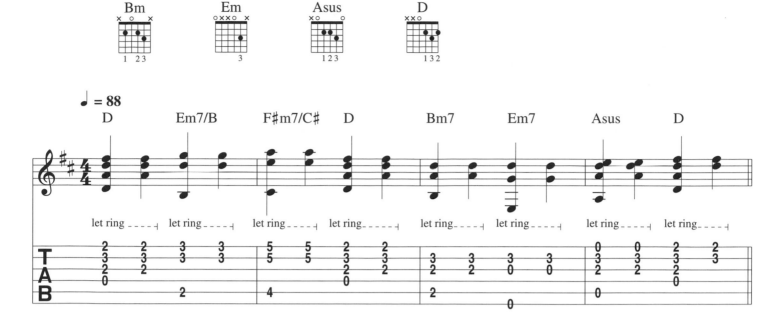

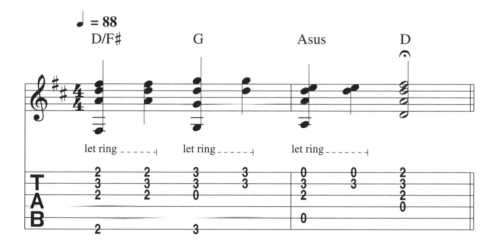

And then you could add the D/F♯, G, Asus, back to D.

⓫ Funkier Chords – Descending Ideas

The key of D has many possibilities and there are other things that we can do to make the chords funkier. If you play the open D string, D and F♯ on the seventh fret of the second and third string, and your open E string you also get a D chord (Dadd9).

Dadd9

Then move to a partial A chord (A/D),

A/D

a partial G Chord (G6/D),

G6/D

and a partial D chord (D5).

D5

When you put them together they sound like this:

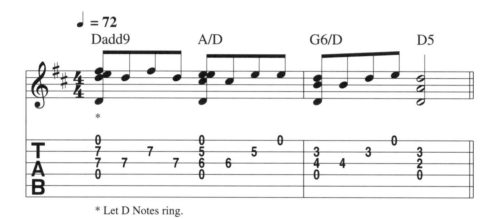

* Let D Notes ring.

It works really nicely as a little descending line.

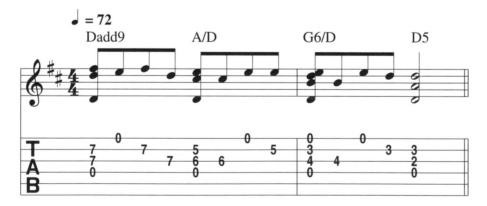

If you are not picking but strumming, it would sound like this:

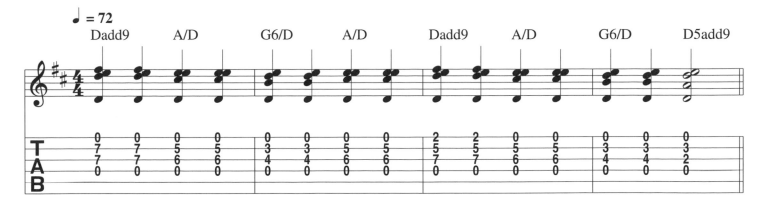

You could start with your D chord, move up to a C/D chord, and resolve it up to D.

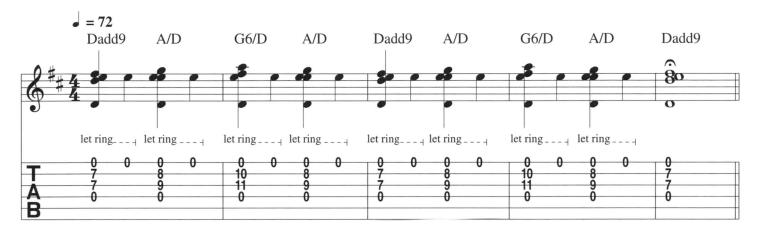

12 Key of E – Three-note Chords and Progressions

Let's move on to the key of E which has its own set of rules and its own set of opportunities. The key of E is really great for some funky chords that are three-note jazz and blues chords. The first position is a B7 chord,

which is moved up to the sixth fret to make E7.

When I remove my pinky from the top string we are left with this:

E7

Within that chord, the three notes that you are fretting form an E7 chord.

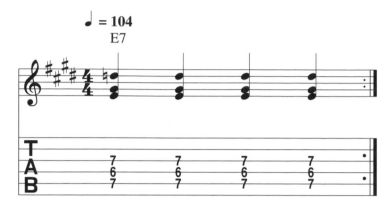

It is true that with this particular chord all of the strings can be played,

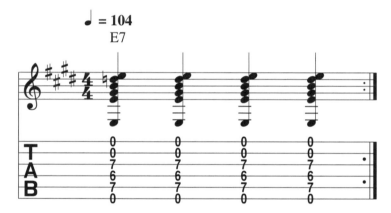

but because this is a movable form you have to be aware not to hit the open strings. For example, you will notice that if you move the chord up one fret to F7 and strum all of the open notes, the chord doesn't work.

The F7 does work when you hit just those three notes.

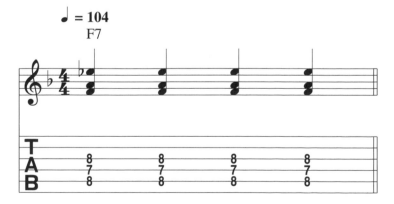

If you think of this as very tight chords with just three notes, you are going to get a lot of use out of this. So here's your E7:

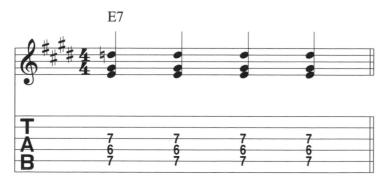

If you were playing a blues, the next chord would be an A7,

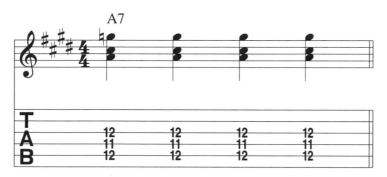

then you would return to E7, jumping back and forth between E7 and A7.

If you take that form and move up to the thirteenth fret you have B7,

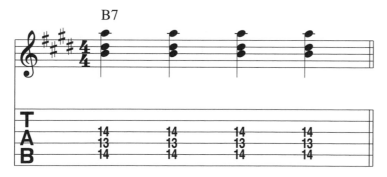

which you can also play in 1st position,

and then back to E.

So if you were to play a blues progression based off these three-note chord forms
in the key of E, it would go like this:

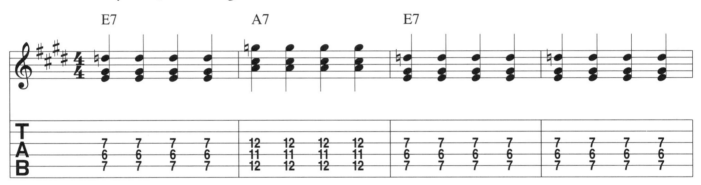

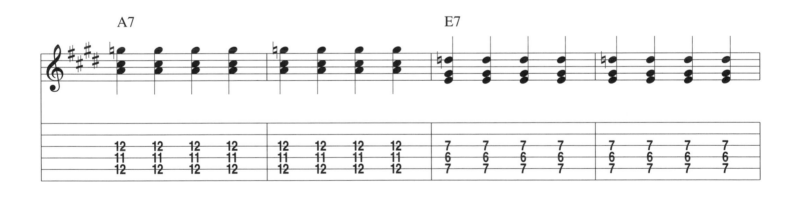

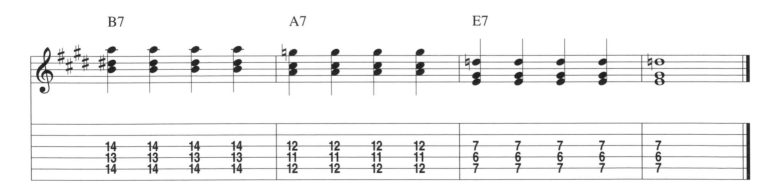

◆13 Three-note Blues and Jazz Chords

Now that works just fine but there is another way to do it that will really expand your chord playing. If you take your first finger and put it on the sixth string - fifth fret, your second finger on the fourth string - fifth fret, and your third finger on the third string - sixth fret, you get an A7 chord.

This is a very movable and tight sounding chord voicing.

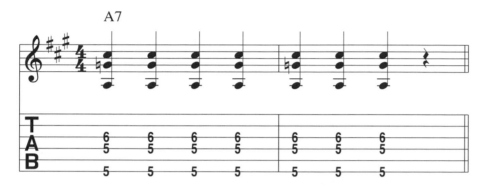

When we move this chord to the seventh position we get B7.

Now the trick is to incorporate the original E7 voicing with these two new voicing for A7 and B7.

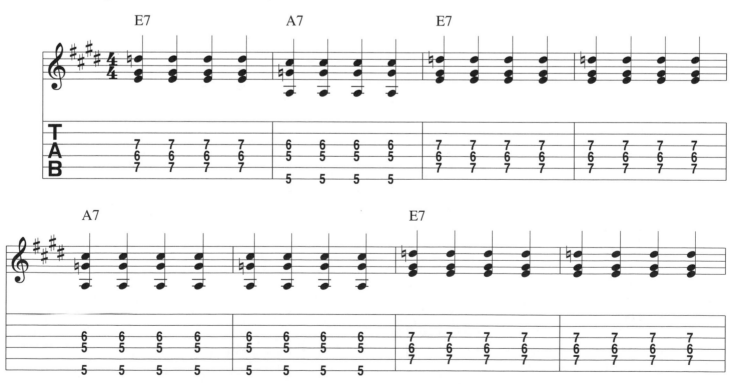

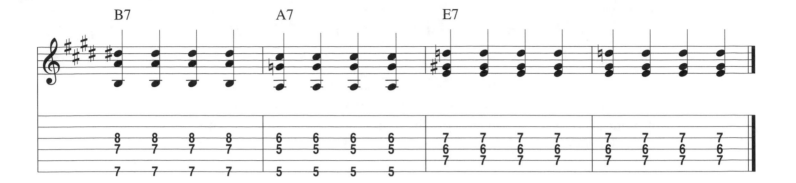

◆14◆ Moving the Chords

Recognizing that the A7 and B7 chords are also movable voicings, you can take your A7 voicing and move it to the twelfth position and play E7.

So here once again is A7, B7, and E7.

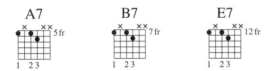

Make sure when you are playing these voicings to dampen the open strings around them.

My favorite way to play these chords with my right hand is to pluck each note using the thumb, first, and second finger of the right hand.

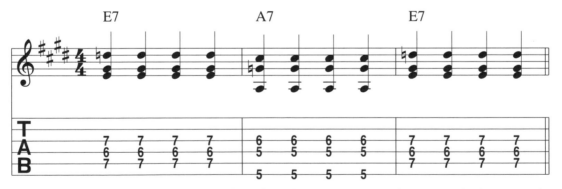

When you are playing the E7 chord with the root on the seventh fret, another possibility is to move your second finger over one string on the same fret and play the note B.

So your bass goes like this.

In conjunction with the chords you get:

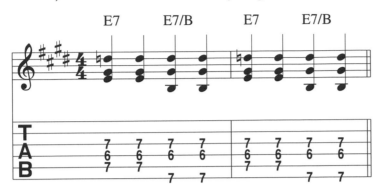

15 Turnaround (Short Version)

The best way to work on these new chords is to practice them as turnarounds.
The following is a common turnaround:

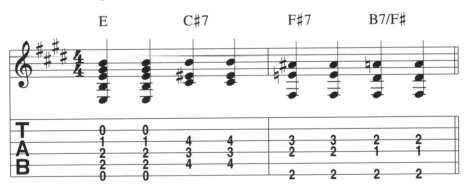

Here is another slight variation on the above example:

◆16 Long Turnaround

One of my very favorite turnarounds incorporates the chords we looked at earlier in this manner:

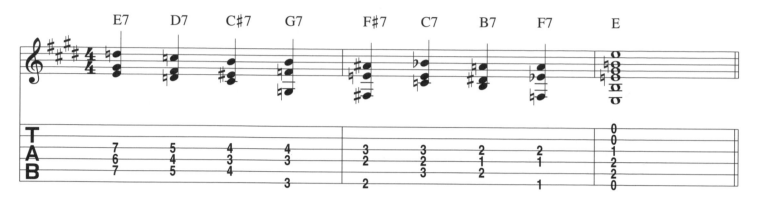

This works great as a turnaround for blues or jazz because it follows the bass line.

◆17 Turnaround #2

Another way to play this turnaround is to begin with E7 in twelfth position and play an almost mirror image of the earlier progression.

E7, D7, C#7, G7, F#7, C7, B7, F7, E7.

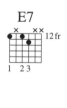

You can play these chords and continue down the neck with the previous progression.

You can play a simpler turnaround in the key of E by doing this:

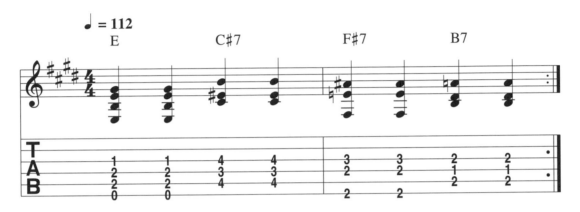

⬥18 Using Chords in Alternate Ways

This leads us to other subtle movements up the neck with these three-note chords.

E, B7, this full E, and maybe going to an A7.

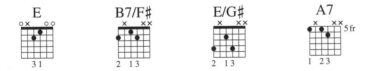

So together we have:

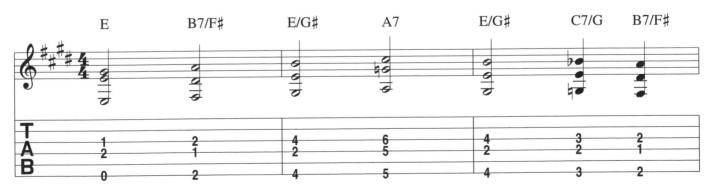

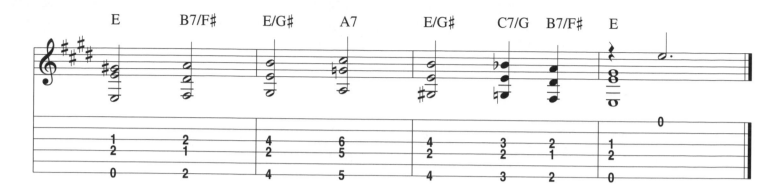

You can also do a simple walk-up that you may have heard in some R&B tunes.

This is really nice going to a C#7, F#7, B7, back to E.

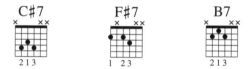

So that progression would be:

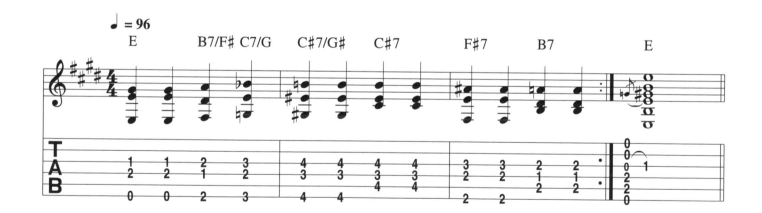

28

⟨19⟩ Review of Other Keys

We can expand these chords simply by adding one other note. This is generally done with the pinky. Take the B7 position and move it up to the seventh fret. Add your pinky to the second string - eighth fret. This chord is called E7#9.

E7#9

This chord can be played in a funky rhythm,

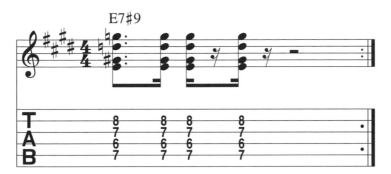

or a more bluesy rhythm. This chord is a movable voicing. The note that is under the second finger is always your root.

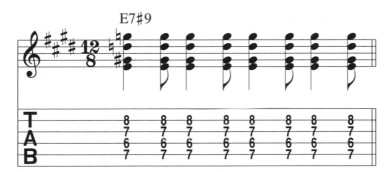

If you take your E7#9 chord and move your fourth finger down one fret you get E9.

E9

If you go to your A7 chord with the root on the sixth string and add your pinky to the second string - seventh fret, you get an A13 chord.

A13

When you flatten your pinky onto the note B on the first string, you get A13 with
the ninth on top.

A13

These chords too are movable voicings.

◆20 Adding Ninths

You should practice all of these turnarounds in other keys. For example, D:

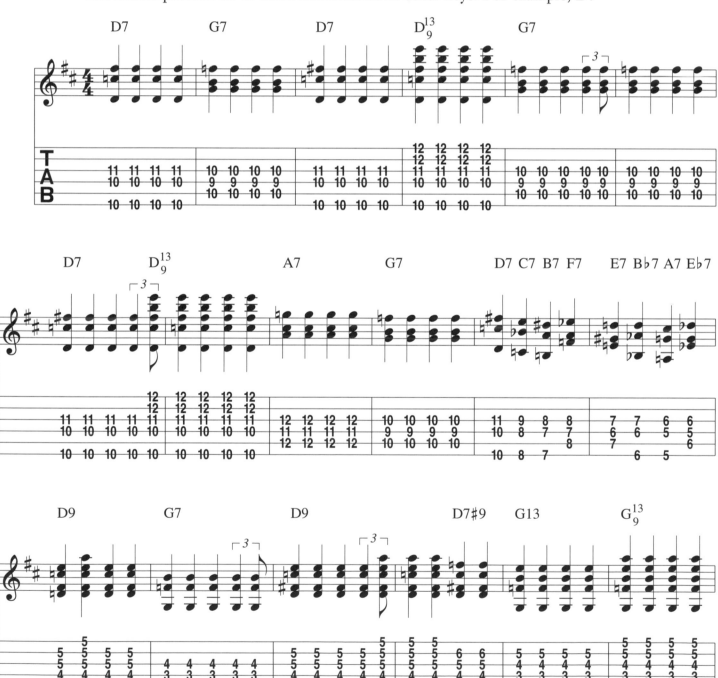

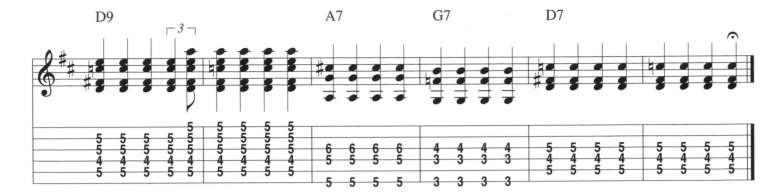

As you continue to study you'll learn how to move these chords around the neck in any key. Soon you'll know that if someone calls a tune in B♭, you can play it here:

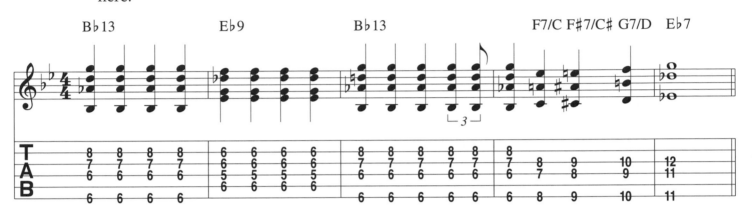

or E♭

By knowing where the root of the chord is and which of the two chord positions to choose from, you should be able to locate any chord that you need.

You should also experiment by adding notes to chords.

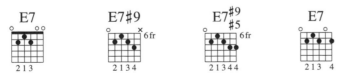

🔷21 Minor Key Chords

Let's take a look at some minor key ideas. Your Em chord looks like this:

By adding your pinky, you get your minor seventh.

By adding your F♯ on the first string - second fret, you get Em9.

You can also play Em7 with a barre chord.

You can also play Em7 as a three-note chord.

🔷22 Using Ninth in Bass and Cadd9

One of the great things about E minor is that you have the open strings to work with. One chord that works well in this fashion is your Em9 chord with the F♯ on the fourth string.

You can then move the B to C and then return to the Em9.

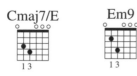

You can also go to a Cadd9 chord.

Cadd9

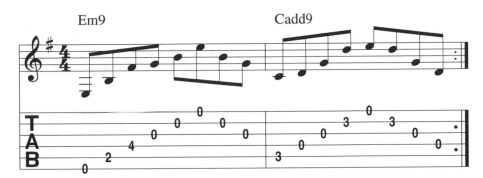

Another great progression is: Em9 – Cadd9 – Am7 – B7sus.

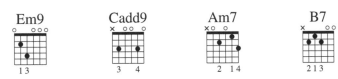

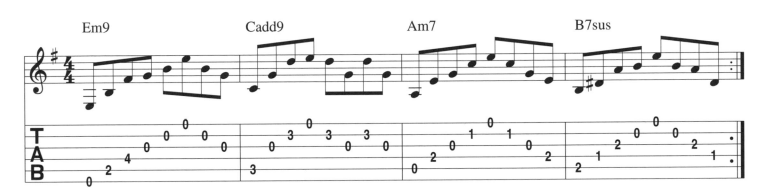

And up the neck it would be:

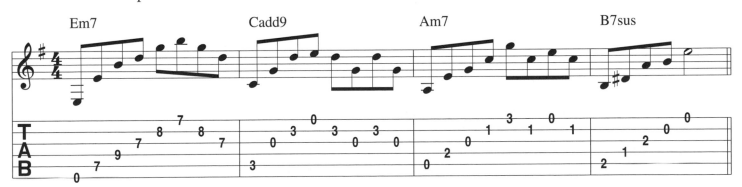

You can also play the Am as a barre.

Am7

You can also add your pinky on the E string to this chord.

Am9   Am7

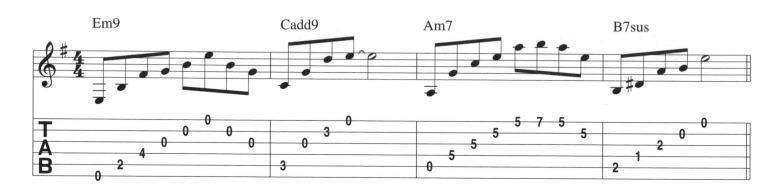

Em9   Cadd9   Am7   B7sus

Expanding Progressions – Am – Bm, Etc.

So to expand your chord knowledge a little more, let's try Am7 – Bm7 – Cadd9 – D – Em9.

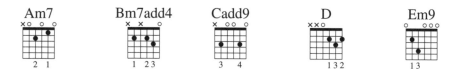

Am7   Bm7add4   Cadd9   D   Em9

You can also play the D/F#.

D/F#

So you can do it like:

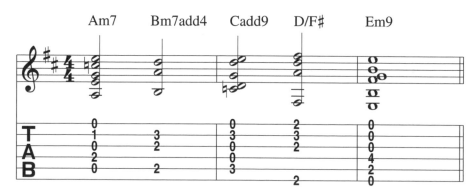

Am7   Bm7add4   Cadd9   D/F#   Em9

or:

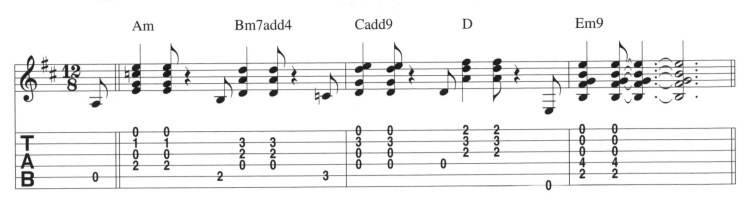

How you play these progressions with your right hand is also very important. You can play it pick style:

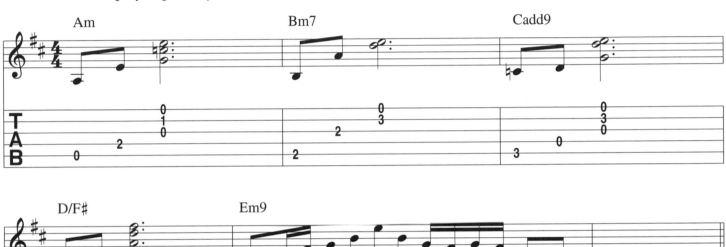

🔹24 G Progression

Another alternate progression would be to go: G – Am7 – Bm7add4 – Cadd9 – F

G

Am7

Bm7add4

Cadd9

F

◆25 E Progression

In the key of E you can also add a ninth in the bass, to F#m7, to G#m7, to an A with a B on top.

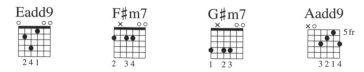

You can play this ascending and descending.

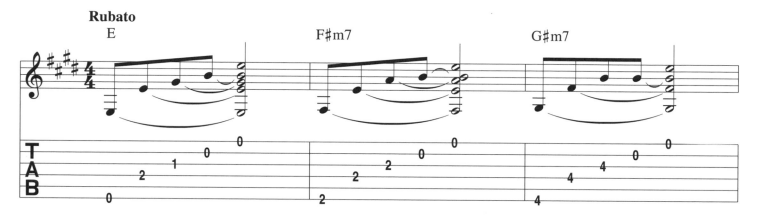

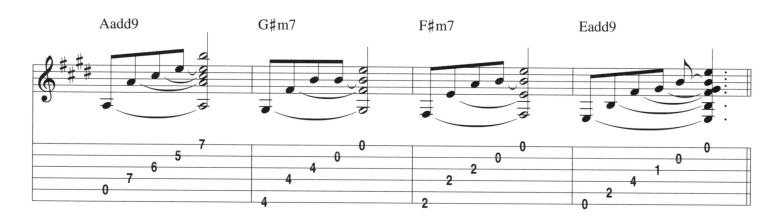

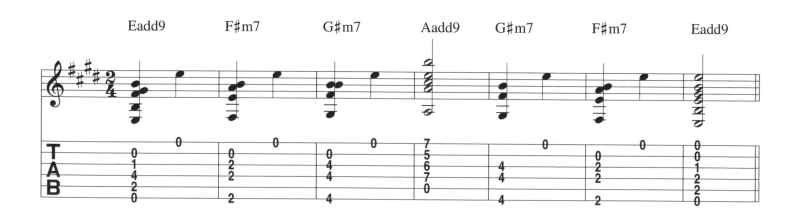

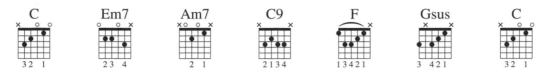

26 C Progression

In the key of C we can play:

and turnaround to G

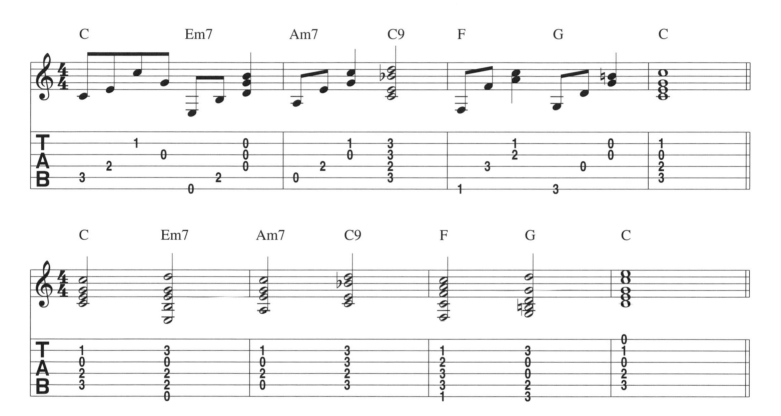

You could also play D/F# in place of C9.

What makes this progression really interesting is the bass movement.

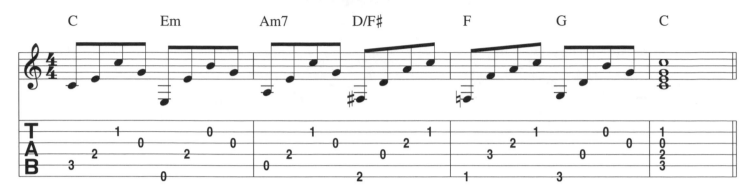

◆27 Two and Three-note Chords

Let's look at some two and three-note movable chords.

You can ascend and descend using these chords:

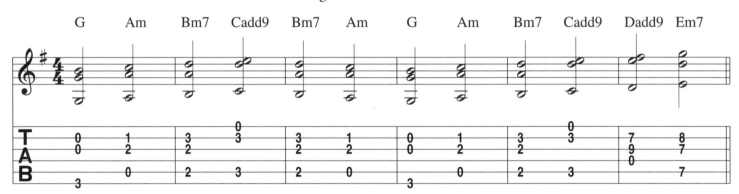

You can also just go up part way:

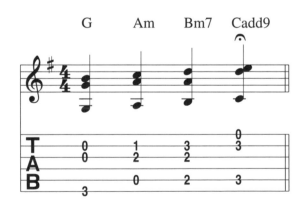

You may also start on the Em:

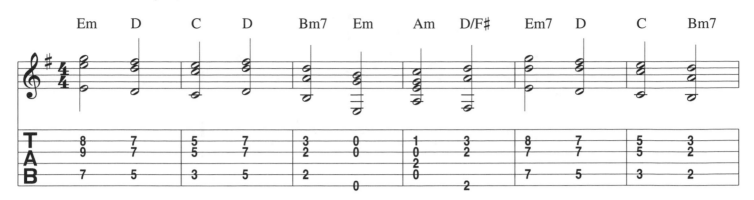

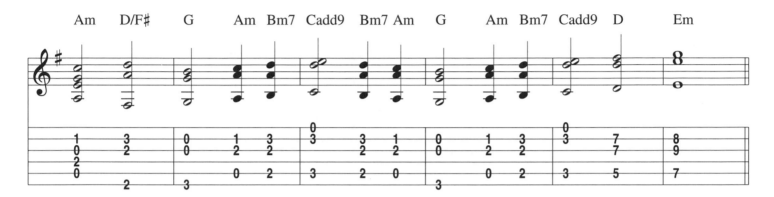

Other chords to look at are ones that take advantage of the open strings. In the key of E you have:

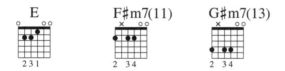

If you were to pluck it:

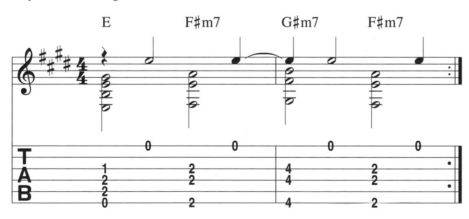

and go to A,

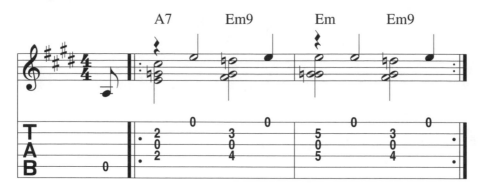

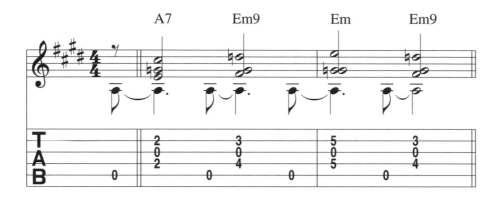

and back to E.

You can also play your E progression and end up on this A chord.

A

◆28 Bluesy Idea

You can also start here on the seventh fret and work down the neck to E.

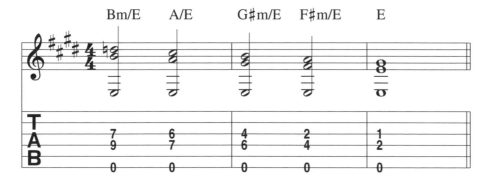

You can also strum these chords being careful not to play the open A string.

The two and three-note chords are really interesting.

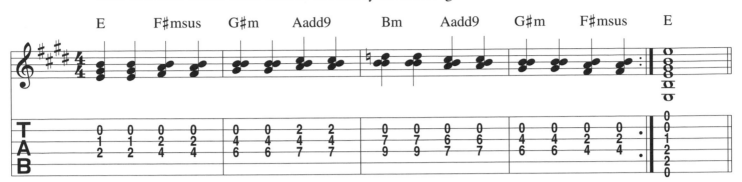

Now chords in other types of turnarounds are effective. Take an E chord, move it up to the fourth fret, and take your third finger off the fourth string. Now you have E7.

If you take this and move it down chromatically you get a turnaround in the key of E.

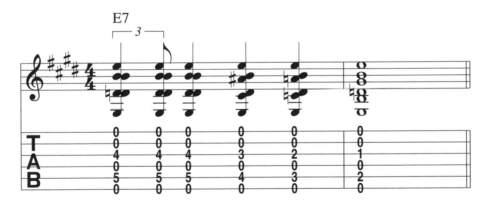

The best way to play this is to lightly dampen the strings you are not playing with the fleshy part of the fingers of your left hand. You can also dampen a bit with the back of the palm of the right hand.

You can also transfer these three-note voicings to the higher strings:

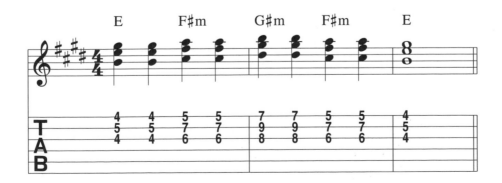

Because your pinky is free, experiment using it to construct melodies.

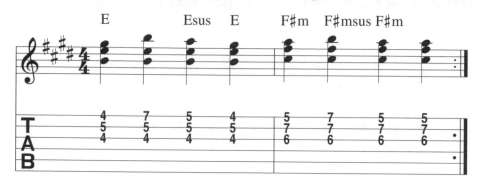

◆30 Major 7 Chords

No lesson on chords would be complete without talking about the Major 7th chord.

Amaj7

With this voicing you can continue up the scale.

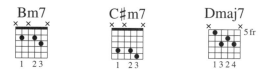

Another Amaj7 voicing is on the fifth fret:

Amaj7

Here are the other chords going up the neck:

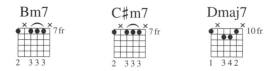

You can also play your minor 7th chords followed by a dominant 9th chord:

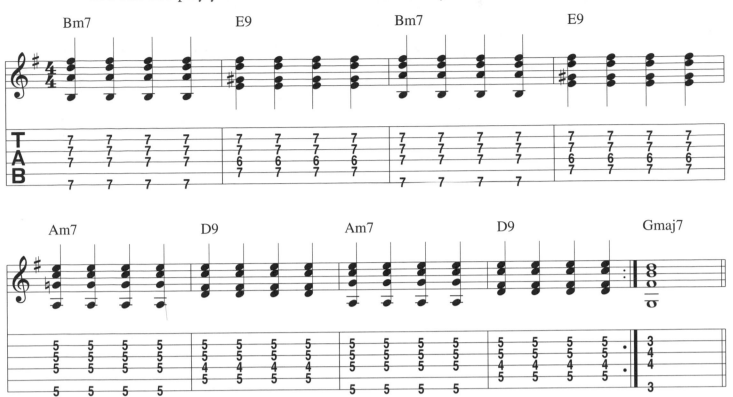

🔷31 Conclusion

I trust that this lesson has been helpful. I'm going to take it out with a little chord playing.

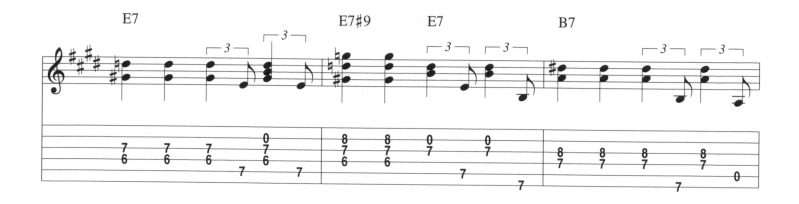

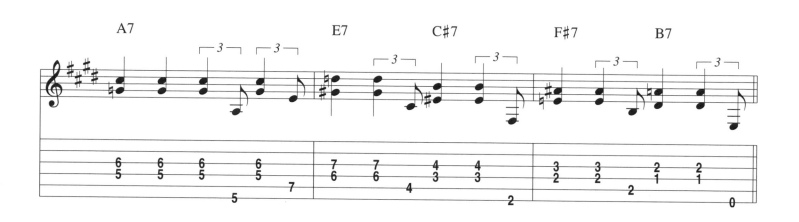

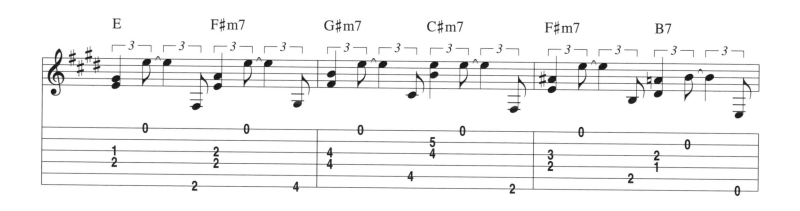

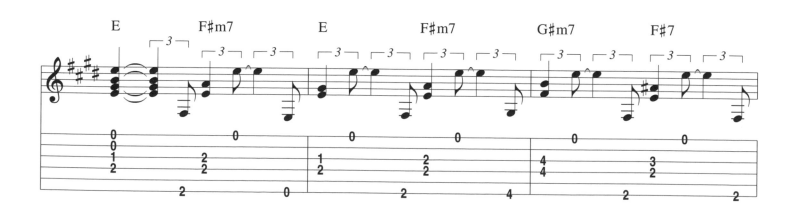

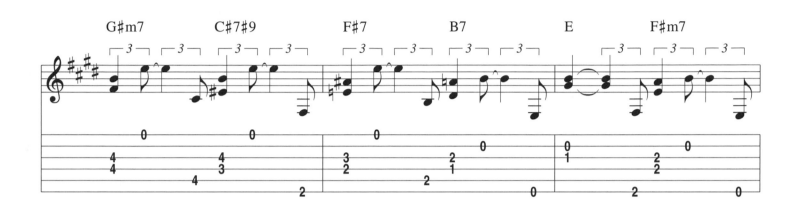

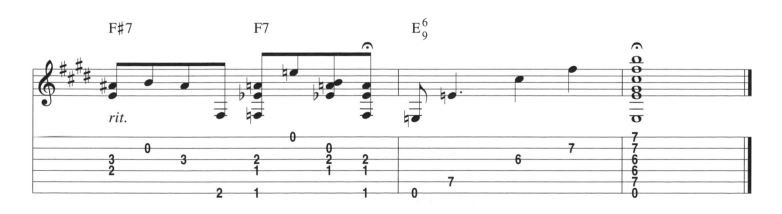

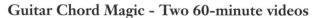

LISTEN & LEARN SERIES

This exciting new series features lessons from the top pros with in-depth CD instruction and thorough accompanying book.

GUITAR

Russ Barenberg Teaches Twenty Bluegrass Guitar Solos
00695220 Book/CD Pack......................$19.95

Keola Beamer Teaches Hawaiian Slack Key Guitar
00695338 Book/CD Pack......................$19.95

Rory Block Teaches Classics of Country Blues Guitar
00699065 Book/CD Pack......................$19.95

Dan Crary Teaches Guitar Flatpicking Repertoire
00695363 Book/CD Pack......................$19.95

Cathy Fink and Marcy Marxer's Kids' Guitar Songbook
00695258 Book/CD Pack......................$14.95

The Guitar of Jorma Kaukonen
00695184 Book/CD Pack......................$19.95

Tony Rice Teaches Bluegrass Guitar
00695045 Book/CD Pack......................$19.95

Artie Traum Teaches Essential Chords & Progressions for Acoustic Guitar
00695259 Book/CD Pack......................$14.95

Artie Traum Teaches 101 Essential Riffs for Acoustic Guitar
00695260 Book/CD Pack......................$14.95

Happy Traum Teaches Blues Guitar
00841082 Book/CD Pack......................$19.95

Richard Thompson Teaches Traditional Guitar Instrumentals
00841083 Book/CD Pack......................$19.95

BANJO

Tony Trischka Teaches 20 Easy Banjo Solos
00699056 Book/CD Pack......................$19.95

MANDOLIN

Sam Bush Teaches Bluegrass Mandolin Repertoire
00695339 Book/CD Pack......................$19.95

HARMONICA

Paul Butterfield Teaches Blues Harmonica
00699089 Book/CD Pack......................$19.95

John Sebastian Teaches Blues Harmonica
00841074 Book/CD Pack......................$19.95

For More Information, See Your Local Music Dealer, or Write To:

HAL•LEONARD®
CORPORATION
7777 W. Bluemound Rd. P.O. Box 13819 Milwaukee, WI 53213

PIANO

David Bennett Cohen Teaches Blues Piano
A Hands-On Course in Traditional Blues Piano
00841084 Volume 1 Book/CD Pack..................$19.95
00290498 Volume 2 Book/CD Pack..................$19.95

Warren Bernhardt Teaches Jazz Piano
Volume 1 – A Hands-On Course in Improvisation and Technique
00699062 Volume 1 Book/CD Pack.................$19.95

Volume 2 – Creating Harmony and Building Solos
00699084 Volume 2 Book/CD Pack.................$19.95

Dr. John Teaches New Orleans Piano
Volume 1 – In-Depth Sessions with a Master Musician
00699090 Book/CD Pack...............................$19.95

Volume 2 – Building a Blues Repertoire
00699093 Book/CD Pack...............................$19.95

Volume 3 – Sanctifying the Blues
00699094 Book/CD Pack...............................$19.95

PENNYWHISTLE

Cathal McConnell Teaches Irish Pennywhistle
00841081 Book/CD Pack..................$19.95

0199